Self-Confidence

Proven Ways to Boost Your Self Confidence, Self Esteem and Overcome Your Fears

Bianca Sutton

Table of Contents

Introduction

Have you ever found yourself staring into a mirror, looking at your body from head to toe and finding something you hate about yourself? Or maybe you are thinking that you're not good enough because you have a certain flaw? It is hard to be confident when you don't love yourself. This book was written as an inspiration to all those feel insecure about themselves. This book will give you tips on how to love yourself and gain confidence in who you are. It doesn't matter if you're fat, skinny, short, or tall; this book will teach you that it doesn't matter what flaws you have because flaws make us unique. By reading this book you will learn what makes you special. It's time to start loving yourself and learning to be more confident.

I know it is hard to be confident and love yourself. This book will teach you how to stop hating yourself and look at others in a positive manner. The main lessons have helped many as insecure as you are now. With these lessons, you can start loving yourself and seeing the true beauty beneath your flaws. It's time to start loving yourself and learning to be more confident.

Your Personal Goal

In this book, there is a section called "What do I want to accomplish?" in which you can write down your personal goal. Your personal goal could be anything, whether starting a new job, getting into a new school, or maybe even becoming an actress or singer. In order to achieve this goal you have to start believing in yourself and love yourself. Why? When people tell you they don't like what you look like or don't think of you as good enough it can really hurt your confidence. Maybe you have a certain flaw you're trying to cover like short arms or maybe your legs are too long for your body. You might think that people won't like you because of this flaw, but if they actually look at the whole package, they should accept you for who you are.

The following are samples of what will help gain self-confidence and loving who you are:

- Being negative about yourself
- Using others as examples of how you should act
- Looking at yourself through the eyes of others (or putting yourself down)

I have learned that it is hard to love myself, and all the things you see in this book are my own experiences. If you read this book and learn from it, I hope that you will gain confidence and love the way you look. This book has really helped me develop self-confidence by helping me quit all those negative things. It's time to start loving yourself and learning to be more confident about who you are. Remember:

- You can't change your flaws: so stop hating yourself for them. Don't be negative about yourself.

- Don't use others as a way of measuring your confidence. Don't see yourself through the eyes of others.
- Who cares what other people think of you? Your only concern should be how you feel in about you.
- Being scared of what might happen tomorrow is not a good reason for avoiding life.
- No one can make you change your mind, all they can do is show you how to go about changing it.

How to achieve self-confidence by following the 5 Rules for Success

It's time to plant some serenity in your life. We all struggle occasionally, but we don't have to live like we're stuck in the mud. Whether you're dealing with a change that brings uncertainty or you just can't shake off that sense of dread, we've put together five rules for building self-confidence – and happiness – so you can move forward into with confidence.

Rule #1: Remember who you are

Nothing can shake confidence faster than being convinced that you a failure. It doesn't matter if you experience a loss of funds, a marriage ending in divorce, or an unexpected job layoff: each one of these can be a wakeup call to remember who you are and what's important in life. Sure, it might take some time to get back on track with money. Is not having that person in your life really all that bad? The real issue is how we respond to change.

Rule #2: Remind yourself of your strengths

No matter how well you think you've dealt with a situation, if you feel overwhelmed, there's a good chance something else is going on. Whether it's the new role that came with the promotion or the extra sadness brought on by your divorce, take time to reflect on what's important.

Rule #3: Become more supportive of others

If you're in a job where the people around you aren't able to express their concerns or needs, learn how to be supportive and let them know they can count on you. Give them the emotional support they need and don't make them feel silly for their problems. If you're going through a difficult time, interacting with others who are also struggling can help you feel like you're not alone, giving you a much-needed dose of perspective.

Rule #4: Take more time for yourself

We all know that we will benefit from more time to ourselves, but there's usually not enough hours in the day to get everything done. That's okay – we don't need perfect balance, but it's important to find ways to reconnect not only when something goes wrong. Don't underestimate how much support you can get when you take some time for yourself to recharge your battery.

Rule #5: Keep things in perspective

We all get down on ourselves for silly reasons at some point. Instead of dwelling on the little things, use what's happening in your life as a reminder to appreciate the bigger picture and take pride in all you have accomplished. There will always be something else coming up that could be even bigger! Life goes on, and it will continue to unfold the way it was meant long after we're gone. It's about appreciating each moment and not waiting until everything is over and done with.

No matter what's going on in your life, we hope these rules will help you tap into your own personal brand of self-esteem and confidence. Self-confidence is often more about who we are and how we feel than the events happening around us, so make time today to learn more about who you really are. You may be surprised how much easier your life will become.

Chapter 1:
What is self-confidence?

Self-confidence is the first requisite to great undertakings.

-Samuel Johnson

S elf-confidence is a powerful, positive trait that can boost nearly every aspect of your life. The more self-confident you feel, the stronger you become in almost everything you do. This chapter will focus on how to develop self-confidence and tap into this awesome power to live your best life now.

To start with, let's look at what expert, Tom Corley, found out about the connection between successful people and high levels of self-confidence. Mr. Corley has studied over 500 wealthy people as part of his research and found that higher self-confidence is a common trait among the wealthy.

People with low self-confidence, on the other hand, are prone to envy and jealousy. They tend to compare themselves to others and become unhappy with what they have achieved. Self-confident people always strive for personal growth and improvement in everything they do. They understand that we all come with talents and abilities that we can cultivate into something great if we put enough time and effort into it.

Mr. Corley also found that higher levels of self-confidence are correlated with creative thinking because highly confident people are able to better imagine future possibilities and act confidently toward them. One of the greatest ways you can build more confidence is to enjoy small successes which reinforce your belief in your abilities.

However, there are reasons why we might not feel as confident as we could be. We all have what I call a "mental blip" - a moment when our minds process new information in such a way as to inspire doubt and uncertainty. This happens to all of us from time to time, and it can be very disheartening. However, having a mental blip is just a blip - a momentary lapse in judgment. It doesn't define you or your personality.

Instead of getting caught up in the emotion of the blip, you can take control and learn from it. You will learn the right thought patterns that will help build self-confidence instead of undermining it.

When you are out in the world, do you often feel like other people are better or more successful than you? It may be tempting to act arrogant and superior just so that no one can take your job away from you. However, the truth is that in most cases we fall victim to our own insecurities. It would be much healthier if we simply acknowledged our own shortcomings and limitations rather than pretending to have skills we don't have. Our ability to be confident doesn't depend upon the opinions of others, but upon our own level of self-belief - a quality that everyone has.

It's very easy to learn how to be more confident. There are certain habits that successful people cultivate to feel good about themselves and their abilities. One of the most important is visualization - the ability to conjure up in your mind a positive image of your future success, and then mentally practice going through the steps you will take to achieve it. This technique requires a degree of imagination, but it helps to keep focus on what is ahead. You won't be distracted by negative thoughts about yourself because you are too busy thinking about what you want in the future.

Do you find that you become more confident as you make progress towards your goals? Are you able to see what needs to be done and then take steps towards achieving it? Are you able to take action and implement the ideas that come to your mind? If so, you know how to become more confident, and this is a good start.

There are other techniques that can help you build confidence in yourself. You may aspire to contribute something great to the world around you - whether through writing, artwork, or some other skillset. Whatever it is that makes your heart race should be your passion, something you go out of your way to achieve.

When you have achieved something or manifested an idea in your head, it will make you feel good about yourself. You'll want to repeat that experience as much as possible so you can enjoy all the benefits of this positive feeling. It may take some time to develop a winning attitude, but once it is there, you'll attract the right people into your life who can help you achieve your goals. Your confidence will blossom and permeate all areas of your life. All that confidence is bound up in the fact that you know yourself well enough to define exactly what it is going to take for you to be successful. You know what works for you, and what doesn't.

You are the best judge of you, so don't let anyone else tell you what you are good at. You've probably been told a few times in your life that you couldn't do this or that. Maybe people told you that you weren't good at math or said that drawling isn't a real art form. These things may have discouraged and even disillusioned you for a while, but it doesn't always have to be this way.

In order to become more confident, you must believe in yourself and your abilities. This doesn't mean that you are cocky or arrogant about it, but that you accept the fact that you are worth something simply because you exist. If we don't cultivate self-awareness and self-belief, we definitely will suffer from low self-esteem.

When this happens, all sorts of negative emotions and thoughts can take hold of our minds. We can get very caught up in the blips of life that seem to knock us down. We tend to think of ourselves as being weak or fragile in some way, and sometimes this becomes a self-fulfilling prophecy. If you feel like a shell of a person, or something less than what you desire, it is time to take charge of your destiny and build more confidence.

It takes time to become self-aware, accept yourself and begin to love yourself. It isn't always easy, but when it all comes together - when you love who you are - then everything seems so much simpler. You won't have such a hard time with relationships, career choices or "who-you-are". Instead of forgetting who you are to fit in somewhere else, you remember who you really are, and that is the best place to start when it comes to becoming more confident.

You won't realize that you can do something until you do it. So go out and do it! Learn how to draw, play the piano, learn a new language, or get one of your hobbies up to a high level - anything is good. If you feel like your horizons are limited, then try something outside your comfort zone. You don't have to do all these things at once or even in any order. But start somewhere and see where it takes you. You'll be surprised at what you can accomplish when there is no self-doubt clouding your mind.

You are far more creative than you realize. When you are in a funk or doubt yourself, you shut down your creativity. The great thing about it all is that it not necessary to draw from the well of inspiration only. You can get it from all around, in your environment. Don't be afraid to draw on your surroundings for inspiration; the sky is green for a reason!

You can empower yourself with these five simple tips that have worked for me and countless others. It isn't easy, but once you get started, if this is something that resonates with you, then continue to learn and grow from within.

It all starts with one small step. I wish you all the success in the world!

Chapter 2:
Effects of Low Self-confidence

L ow self-confidence can be debilitating. People with low self-confidence often have trouble reaching their full potential at work, in relationships, and even in their own self-development. With their lack of enthusiasm about life, they are less likely to look for new opportunities or try new things. One study found that people with low self-confidence earned on average $9000 less a year from the same position than someone with high confidence would earn.

Since the 1960s, researchers have examined the link between low self-confidence and a wide range of difficulties and problems. In general, these studies have found a connection between feeling insecure about oneself and experiencing difficulty in areas such as school, work, romantic relationships, and conflict resolution. However, researchers have not always been able to establish clear cause-and-effect relationships. But we know that people with a poor performance review from supervisors are more likely to develop low self-confidence than the other way around.

An experiment was done on how low self-confidence affects decision making during competition. Researchers found that participants with low self-confidence were more likely to make decisions based on chance than the participants who had high self-confidence. They also found that the decision to "play it safe" by avoiding risky decisions increased as people experienced a decrease in their perceived competency.

Low self-confidence has been linked to social anxiety, depression, and reduced job performance. Low self-esteem is also correlated with increased likelihood of suicide attempts and suicidal ideation. The various causes of low self-esteem are not fully known; however, researchers have identified potential factors associated with lower levels of self-esteem, including gender, age, social competition (competition with others), and genetics.

Many people believe that low self-confidence is a temporary problem that will eventually resolve itself, and it may be possible to effectively boost self-confidence through some short-term approaches such as building on past accomplishments or finding ways to look forward to new challenges. However, some psychotherapeutic approaches have been shown to be effective at helping people "overcome" their low levels of self-esteem and develop higher levels of self-confidence.

Determining how much a person values their own skills is an important first step in helping people with low self-confidence. In one study, participants who rated themselves high on competence were more likely to feel confident in their abilities than those who rated themselves low on competence. These findings indicate that when people feel confident in their abilities, they become more satisfied and more likely to value themselves.

For many years, people believed that negative self-reflection (i.e., comparing oneself unfavourably to others) was a key factor in the development of low self-esteem, but a recent study suggests that this is not the case. Self-evaluation is not necessarily a predictor of low self-esteem. Rather, this study found that how others evaluate you can be an important factor—specifically if other people tend to view you highly or poorly (based on their perception of your competence). These findings show that it is not the way others view your competence that matters; rather, it is how highly you evaluate yourself. Research has also shown that perceived competence is the most important factor in determining self-esteem. People with lower levels of perceived competence tend to have significantly lower levels of self-esteem than people with higher levels of perceived competence.

In one study, researchers found that when people overestimated their own ability to complete a task (i.e., when they believed they were more competent than the other participants), their feelings of low self-esteem decreased significantly—even though they did not actually perform worse than the other participants. These findings suggest that feeling more confident may actually lead to better performance and, thus, higher self-esteem. One way to build these feelings of self-confidence is through positive self-talk. Positive self-talk involves thinking about oneself in a positive way (e.g., "I am a good listener"), which ultimately help build feelings of self-worth and confidence.

Individuals with low self-confidence often have difficulty controlling their anxiety because they believe that the negative outcome they fear is inevitable. To increase confidence levels in these situations, it is necessary to gain control over their anticipatory anxiety so they can reduce their belief that negative outcomes are inevitable. Reducing negative thoughts about upcoming events may be accomplished through visualizations and other forms of mental rehearsal. Mental rehearsal involves thinking through upcoming events in a positive way and imagining how one could handle difficult situations. This technique can help reduce the self-doubt or negative thoughts that make it difficult for an individual to utilize their skills and abilities effectively.

The most effective way to boost self-confidence is to engage in activities that make people feel they are capable at handling their daily responsibilities as well as tackling new, unfamiliar challenges. These activities may help increase one's sense of competency and self-esteem, as well as boost motivation and the desire to perform at a high level in other areas of life. Some examples of high-confidence builders include exercising, staying organized, reading a good book, volunteering for a cause, helping someone in need, or eating healthy foods.

A study looking into the effects of self-confidence on individual behavior found that confidence can be learned through feedback. When people receive positive feedback about their ability to complete tasks or address a situation effectively, they gain self-confidence and are more likely to succeed in future attempts. On the other hand, when people receive negative feedback about their ability to complete tasks or address a situation effectively, they often become angry and doubt their abilities.

Research has shown that negative feedback can decrease an individual's motivation as well as self-confidence, which can make it more difficult for them to achieve success. Therefore, learning how to receive positive feedback about one's skill in a stressful situation is one important way of boosting confidence levels in these types of situations.

One of the most common causes of low self-confidence is a poor body image (i.e., a negative view of one's appearance). When people are faced with obstacles that cause anxiety or stress, they often focus on their perceived flaws to reduce this anxiety. Anxiety about physical appearance may translate into anxiety about one's abilities as well. If an individual feels they are physically unattractive, it can make them more likely to avoid social situations and volunteer work opportunities, which can affect their self-esteem.

People often rely on the opinions of others to evaluate their self-worth or value as a human being. When people find themselves in unexpected stressful situations (e.g., public speaking), they often focus on these negative remarks that tend to bring them down. However, to build confidence when dealing with stressful situations, one must learn how to ignore these comments and focus on their own performance rather than the judgments of others. If people focus on their own performance first and foremost, they are less likely to feel as though they have failed.

Self-confidence is a skill that can be developed over time, but like any skill, there are several factors that influence how much time it takes to develop it. One of the most influential factors is the amount of respect that others show. If others respect an individual's abilities, they will have a more positive attitude about their capabilities and this self-image will translate into their everyday lives. Self-confidence can also be influenced by relationship dynamics with significant others (e.g., romantic partners) and family members (e.g., parents). Also, self-confidence can be affected by environmental cues (e.g., media messages) and physical obstacles (e.g., genetics).

There are many situations in which people experience stress. A variety of stressors can cause genuine concern for an individual's well-being, but negative or unrealistic beliefs about the self can lead to "stressful" situations that have little or no positive effects. A person may recognize a perceived threat to who they are as a person, but this recognition is not always accurate and serves as poor justification for the individual's emotional response.

Stress may come from external or internal sources. External stressors include issues such as: family problems, financial difficulties, physical illness, or injury, etc. Internal stressors include psychological disorders such as anxiety disorders, depression, and personality disorders. If not properly managed and treated, these disorders can cause a great deal of stress. There are people who have suffered at some point in their lives due to other people's actions which may have resulted in trauma.

In addition to the factors that encourage individuals to construct more negative perceptions of the world around them, it is also important to recognize that stress can be a cause of social isolation. In some cases, when an individual is likely to contact a healthcare professional due to symptoms of stress, they will undoubtedly be experiencing related the physical symptoms of mental health issues.

Self-confidence is sometimes considered to be a reflection of self-esteem, despite the fact that they are not the same thing. To have a high level of self-confidence in one area of life (e.g. work) does not necessarily mean that self-confidence is also high in another area (e.g., relationships). Rather, it seems more likely that a person who has low levels of general self-confidence may not feel confident in many areas of his or her life.

In many cases, a person may lack self-confidence in some area of his or her life and not know exactly why. They may be reluctant to seek the help that they need to overcome their problems because of the negative connotations that this may bring to other areas. For example, if a person is only confident when he or she is with others (e.g., work) but not confident when talking to them (e.g. friends), this may mean that the person doesn't feel confident on a relationship level.

The person might be unsure how to improve their levels of self-confidence, leading them to avoid people and situations. This lack of confidence may be caused by external factors such as past experiences that fed low self-esteem.

Chapter 3:
Build up your self-confidence by Boosting your Self-esteem!

S elf-esteem is different from self-confidence. Some people believe they have high self-esteem but as a matter of fact, they just feel good about themselves because someone told them how great they are or something good has happened in their lives. On the other hand, self-confidence comes from knowing that you are worth it. You have inner security, and this gives you a sense of accomplishment.

A good example can be found in children: they believe they can do anything, and their role models matter to them. As they grow older, they start to understand that someone was telling them what to do instead of their own minds guiding them. This is why we should not count on the opinion of others as an indicator or our self-esteem but rather rely on ourselves and our own abilities to succeed in whatever we do! Otherwise, we will remain where we are until someone else comes along and pushes us further. In our minds, self-esteem is tied directly with self-confidence. When we believe in ourselves and our abilities, this gives us a sense of security that other people will not be able to take from us.

How to build up the self-esteem?

There are many ways to increase your self-esteem and the steps will vary for everyone: some people find it helpful to have a mentor or someone to support them through their development stages. Others struggle with voices inside their heads, telling them that they are not good enough, which creates anxiety. You should set goals that give you confidence as it accelerates your growth over time.

There are many things that people do to boost their self-esteem like going to the gym, eating healthy, or working on their hobbies. It all depends on what will work for you and the best thing is to try one after another until you find one that helps develop your self-confidence as soon as possible.

Build up your self-confidence by boosting your self-esteem!

In life, there are many things we can learn do to increase our self-confidence because it is not something that comes naturally It is a skill we need to learn and from the very beginning. Think of it as a certain behavior instead of an irreversible part of us. We should also try to do new things and be open to different people as this will make it easier to focus on other things instead of staying in our comfort zone. If you want quick results, then you need to find someone who believes in you and supports your decisions.

Low Self-Esteem

There are a lot of reasons to have low self-esteem. A person can be too hard on themselves, or they might not know enough about themselves to feel good about themselves. Mental illness such as depression can decrease self-esteem. If you're not feeling positive about yourself, it's difficult to live in the moment; you may be inclined to focus on what you don't have rather than what you do have.

Confidence should be thought of as a positive trait that allows people to believe in themselves and their abilities. A true sense of confidence can help someone accept themselves for who they are and what they have. But a lack of confidence can leave someone afraid to take risks and try new things.

Confidence is more than just having faith in oneself. It's also about acting on it. This isn't to say that a person who isn't confident needs to go out and get a boost from an extreme sport like sky diving or bungee jumping. But if the person feels good about life, they should take steps towards bettering themselves by trying new things or furthering their education to advance in their career field.

If you're lacking confidence in yourself, it's time to get out there and meet people. Take some chances even if you fear rejection. If you don't take chances and push yourself to do things you're not comfortable with, you'll never know if living outside your comfort zone is best for you. As far as job and career advancement go, most jobs are competitive. It never hurts to do some research on your talents or skill set so you can be better prepared than the next person when an opportunity presents itself.

Everyone has low points in life. They might not be living up to their own standards, but that doesn't mean they feel inferior. If someone feels inferior just because of their situation, they should do some work to fix themselves up before it affects the people around them negatively.

The point is not to give up and flounder, but to know that you can get help and there is a lot to do on your own. There are certain attitudes to adopt and areas to avoid as listed below.

1.) Don't give in to peer pressure: This is a big one because if you don't speak out, people will assume that it's okay to do whatever they want no matter what anyone else thinks about it. If, however, we respect each other and condemn negative peer pressure, then we have a chance to live in a world where everyone is happy and equal. This is especially true for sexuality and racism.

2.) Don't be too picky with your work schedule: I know this may sound a little obvious, but it's something that people struggle with on a regular basis. An overloaded work schedule means they don't get any time to themselves. I can understand not wanting to give up all of your free time, but you'll find that it is possible for both work and life to fit into your schedule.

3.) Don't scrimp on necessities: If you find yourself struggling with money, there are some things you need to stop doing right away. It's not only about cutting back on certain things like eating out or going out when you don't have enough money in the bank, but also what's called a financial diet. This means you should stop spending money on things you don't need like magazines or costly coffee drinks in the morning. You'll start to feel better when you're not wasting money on things that aren't important to your health and your goals.

4.) Don't be afraid of reaching out for help: You can't do it all alone and that's okay. If you need help, ask someone close to you. I know it's difficult to admit that you can't do it all by yourself but if anyone proves this point, it's me. I didn't ask for help until I had graduated college and started looking for a job in my field.

5.) Don't be afraid to take some time off: If you start taking breaks, it will only benefit you in the long run. The more you work yourself into the ground, the less likely you'll stop, sit back, and reflect on how your life is progressing. It will also keep you from feeling overwhelmed when meeting new people - something many struggle with.

6.) Don't bring shame on yourself: It's okay to admit when you don't know something or someone knows more about an issue or topic. You won't feel as embarrassed if others around you know that this isn't your strong suit. It's better to be considered a person that everyone can ask than the person who pretends they know everything.

7.) Don't worry about other people's opinions: You are you, and it doesn't matter if you don't impress or even falls short of someone else's expectations. If you don't like what you're doing and someone out there can make a difference in your life, then find them and encourage yourself to be better today than you were yesterday. But if someone makes fun of you or tries to judge your actions, then just look them straight in the eye and ask if they feel that way based on their own experiences.

8. Don't follow the "norm" of your peers: It's okay not to be everyone's best friend. You don't have to go out every night and drink every weekend just because your friends do. The same goes for clubs, bars, and even going home with someone who happens to catch your eye. There is a big difference between someone who is making healthy decisions and someone out looking for trouble. It's okay to be single but you should also be smart about it, especially if you want to meet someone you have more in common with.

9. Don't feel the need to hold everything in: It can be stressful when you're going through a stressful time in your life. We all have them and if we don't talk about them, it can build up inside, making us resentful toward the people that we love. If

you're having an issue with something and it's making you feel bad or depressed, you should open up to someone to help you work through it.

10. Don't let others dictate the way you live your life: There are many things you can do for yourself. If you work out so hard that your heart is beating 100 miles a minute, then it's okay to take a break and walk around the block once or twice if you're feeling tired. You can eat whatever you want without everyone judging. If going out to drink doesn't interest you, don't do it just because everyone else is. And if spending all of your extra money on yourself is making your bank account feel like a bottomless pit, then cancel some of those automatic payments and put the money toward something that will make your life better.

In all honesty, if we all follow this list, the world would be a much nicer place. There are a lot of good and bad traits that each person possesses, and we just have to figure out how to combine them to live happy lives. So listen to these tips and try them out on your own because everyone else will thank you for it.

Chapter 4:
The power of Self-image

T here are a lot of things in life that may make you feel bad about yourself. Your life could be going downhill, and maybe people are making fun of you, saying you're just not good enough. You might have low self-esteem and don't believe in your abilities, and, most importantly, you don't believe in yourself.

None of these issues can overshadow the importance of believing in yourself. We are all unique and have different qualities. We start experiencing more self-confidence when we believe in what we know about ourselves. For sure, this might not be the answer to all your problems, but it's an essential part to any success you seek in your life.

An example is a woman who believed she was a bad mother and harmed her children because of it. Another example is an individual who believed he wouldn't have a good job because of past issues with money management. He suffered many losses so he believed he could never make money again.

But when you put your belief in yourself, you are building a strong foundation for yourself and your life. If you believe that you can do something, there is nothing stopping you! Make sure that the decisions you make with your life are based on facts and not assumptions.

For example, the individual who has a lot of trouble handling money blamed himself about his past mistakes. He believed that he was always going to fall short of every single goal he had because of his attitude. He couldn't see beyond what had happened in his past so he couldn't trust himself or anyone else anymore.

It is very important to know that every person deserves a second chance and the will to improve. Instead of looking at our mistakes, we should look at what we have learned from them instead. We can use the lessons we've learned as a guide for the future so we won't fall into the same pit again.

Our beliefs are powerful because they are one of the most important factors that drive us toward our goals in life. Depending on your beliefs, you can either set yourself up for success or set yourself up for failure. A positive belief is something that encourages you to be more productive and successful. If you believe that you can make it through all the challenges in life, that will give you the strength to overcome them! But on the other hand, a negative belief can make things much worse for you.

If we have a negative belief like, "I don't deserve to be happy" or "I will fail again, I try and fail again," then in those moments where we are feeling down and miserable, our negative beliefs will definitely come true. This is because our current circumstances are not within our control. We start blaming ourselves and tend to believe everything that others say about us.

We have to find new ways of eliminating negative beliefs from our minds. It's not easy to take away a belief in yourself, but it's an essential part of the process. You just need a simple exercise.

1. write down your negative belief

2. write down why it's bad for you

3. finally, write down what you can do about this belief

For example: "I feel like I can never get my things done in time" or "I feel like my work is always so useless", etc. Then, "It makes me feel like I am not good enough. It makes me feel like I'm useless. It leads me to procrastinate so much. It really frustrates me when other people can do things when I can't," etc.

Now what you can do about that belief to change it into a positive one. Find a way that you can improve that belief in your life by replacing it with something positive and motivating. For example, "I can set a realistic plan for myself to get things done in time. I can learn ways to improve my work, so it seems more valuable and useful. I will try to be more patient with myself when I am feeling frustrated or annoyed with my progress so that I don't give up," etc.

For a better result, do this exercise regularly until you start seeing positive results. You can also ask for help from a friend or family member you trust.

Why you shouldn't let people control your self-image

Although we have to be responsible for ourselves, we can't stop people from saying negative things about us. This is because no one's judgment is perfect, and it can easily be proved wrong. You have to make sure that you don't let people bring you down and end up feeling bad about yourself. That's why, to avoid this kind of problem, learn how to control our self-image in a healthy manner.

But first of all, you need to realize that your perception of reality is not the same as someone else's; and that's why everyone has a different view of life. Many people believe that they have a perfect life despite the fact that other people see their lives as a mess.

Then many people are convinced of their superiority over others while others who believe they have no talents at all. People like this tend to feel bad about themselves and even the things around them. This attitude will not only make their lives miserable, but it will also ruin the image people have of them. So, you should know how to improve your self-image in a healthy way so that your self-esteem won't be diminished by negative perceptions from other people.

One of the ways you can change your perception about yourself is by analysing what you do well and your strengths. In other words, you should know where you stand in this world so you can be proud of yourself and your talents. Another way that will help you accept yourself is to realize how different everyone is in the world. Everyone has their own problems and things they are unhappy with in life, although they may appear normal to others around them. So, it's important to understand that everyone has his or her own problems that makes everybody special and unique.

A third way to improve our self-image is the way we think about ourselves. Most of us have the wrong perception of ourselves which keeps us from feeling good about our lives. If you're going to stop thinking bad thoughts about yourself, you need to make a conscious effort of how you think about your life.

The last way to improve your self-esteem is by making a conscious effort to improve something in your life. Even if it's just little thing, it would be considered something significant and valuable for someone who holds an important place in this world.

These are just some of the many ways you can improve your self-perception. By practicing mew habits, you can start to feel better about yourself and the world around you. This will give you a big boost in your self-esteem and help make life better.

If you have an issue with your self-image, then what you need now is to improve your self-esteem by practicing the steps above. These steps will help us on our journey toward a healthier self-perception so we can live happy lives. The power of positive thinking is huge, and you should always use it to achieve your self-improvement goals. So, give these steps a try and see for yourself the kind of impact they can have in improving how you see yourself.

Chapter 5:
Goal Setting and Action Planning

W hen it comes to self-confidence, there are many ways to help yourself and begin the process of building confidence. You might be someone who has led a tough life so far and has battled with low self-confidence for a long time. Or you might be someone who is feeling as though they don't have enough going for them, and these feelings have started to influence how you feel about yourself. Either way, this chapter will give you an idea of some steps to take to build your confidence.

The first thing we should tackle is goal setting and action planning: if we work on our goals every day, it becomes easier to see our progress. If we don't see our progress, it is easy to become demoralized and feel as though we aren't making any at all. By working on your goals every day, you can keep yourself motivated to get the result you want.

Start by setting a goal you would like to achieve right now. This goal can be about improving your self-confidence level. It is not enough just to set a goal; if it is just words on paper, it does not mean anything. You must take tangible steps every day to help yourself reach these goals if you want them to be effective and make a difference in your life.

The first step is to identify what you can do. For example, you might set a goal to get a new job interview every day. So every day, you must dress well, go for the interview, and ensure that your CV is up to date and accurate. If no suitable positions are advertised on sites like Indeed or Monster, you can speak with your manager about opportunities within your company or search online for job openings in your area.

Then, write down your plan and create a series of steps to fulfill your goal. You might set a goal to get two job interviews every month. This means you have to book one interview and then wait for the response before scheduling another one. Or you might set a new goal of getting interviewed by different companies every month. You can create an action plan but give it time; if nothing happens in just one day, it will be easy to get discouraged or feel you are not making any progress. Although this is all about self-improvement, it can be easy to get side-tracked by other goals that do not help the progress you are trying to make.

For example, it is a good idea to set goals like getting more hours at work or earning more money so you can pay your bills, but these are not about improving your self-confidence. These types of goals should be set in small steps over time and not within a short period of time.

Another thing to keep in mind is that setting goals and action plans does not mean losing sight of other important aspects of your life. You must remember that you have other responsibilities and tasks to complete on top of building your confidence. Thus, it is important that you stay focused on these everyday rather than letting them go entirely.

By setting goals and action plans, you will see your progress and feel more motivated. If you can measure your progress each day, you will know how much you are contributing to the change in your life. Your confidence will grow as time goes on, giving you more motivation to continue working hard and taking steps toward achieving the goals important to you.

Achievement of self-confidence is necessary. If we don't believe in ourselves, we will never achieve our dreams. So, it is very important to improve our self-confidence. We need to get rid of all the barriers that are holding us back and help ourselves on the way to achieving anything we do not like. This step must be started with an attitude that it is possible for to improve the things in our lives that are less than great. There are many ways to improve your self-confidence and you must decide what concerns you the most.

If we use our energy and time in the best way, if we will learn how to manage ourselves, if we will cultivate a positive attitude and learn how to deal with the problems of others, then we will achieve self-confidence. This kind of confidence is not about getting these or those things. It is about being confident in oneself as well as being confident that one can help others. You must know that it <u>takes a lot of patience, determination, and effort</u> to become more self-confident or secure. Only through self-confidence can you see that you have the ability to achieve your goals and make yourself happy.

How to get rid of self-doubt?

Self-doubt is the shadow that covers our hearts, and we have all been brought up thinking it is a bad thing. We are told to always be perfect and never fail, but why? The first reason why we often fail is because of our fear of failing. Whenever we begin any task or venture, there will be some doubts about whether it will succeed or not. But if we allow this doubt to take over, it would be extremely difficult to ever succeed in anything again. We have to all learn that there is no shame in not being good at something. We must realize the importance of self-doubt and be okay with it. It is a normal thing, but it is never a healthy situation for doubt to take over your mind and make you believe you cannot succeed.

<u>Everyone has his or her own doubts,</u> but the only difference between successful people and those who never achieve anything significant is that they do not let self-doubt control them. If you allow something bad to happen to you, then naturally you will feel bad. But if you can get over this and not allow it to hold you back, you will see that it is not so bad. Most people do not realize that their self-doubt and fears are holding them back from achieving their dreams.

For many people, <u>fear of failure is the biggest obstacle</u> to overcome. This negative feeling makes everyone believe in failure and they fail to start something even if they have the desire to do so. Others choose a life of self-destruction because they are scared of the consequences of failing. If we really want to change our lives for better, we need to get rid of these feelings of fear or doubt inside us.

What is so great about self-doubt?

If we want to achieve anything in life, then we must get rid of self-doubt. It may seem like an impossible task because it is a part of our minds. But believe me that there is one way to solve this problem, and it involves changing your mentality. To do this, you need to understand the real problem and how self-doubt affects every aspect of your life. If you believe you can do something bad or wrong, then this will not only affect your daily decisions but also make you doubt your abilities in everything you do. It comes to such a point that you are scared to do anything, and you just sit back. This is an unfortunate aspect of self-doubt and the main reason why many people do not achieve their goals.

While some people find it hard to be themselves, others simply lack the talent required, and they have no idea how to change this. But when you let this self-doubt control your life, it becomes a huge health risk. In order to stop self-destructing, many people start feeling depressed, even more than before because they do not understand how things could go wrong and what the next step should be. They are afraid of making decisions and even if they do, they usually opt for the safest thing possible. This is a big problem because this keeps them stuck in the same place all the time.

But enough of self-doubt problems. Here are some steps you can take in order to get rid of them once and for all:

Don't put yourself down – I know that this may seem like a cliché, but if you want to feel different about yourself, you need to be different first and foremost. People are always putting themselves down and wondering how others see them. Researchers have found that people who do this and compare themselves to others are likely to have a harder time accepting compliments.

Give yourself a break – It is hard to stay positive when everyone around you is falling apart. Life can be stressful, and no one wants to be surrounded by it, but there is no denying that stress makes for unhappiness. If you are not happy with the way your life is currently going, then change it, but don't put so much pressure on yourself and make you feel like everything needs to be perfect. Let go of whatever stresses you may have and embrace the good in life instead.

Don't be a perfectionist – Last but not the least, you must learn not to be a perfectionist. It is okay if you want to make your life perfect but at the same time, it is important you do not let it control you. Use your energy in other ways and accept whatever happens instead of making situations out of them. A lot of people who try to achieve perfection in all things fail because they are stressed out and over-thinking everything. Let go and focus on the things that are important, like taking care of yourself and improving every day instead.

These tips that worked for me, and I am sure they can help anyone else, too. Sure, it may be difficult to get rid of this self-doubt in such a short period of time, but if you keep at it and take your time, you will succeed.

Chapter 6:
What Should we do to Have Self-confidence?

D o what you feel in your heart to be right - for you'll be criticized anyway. You'll be damned if you do, and damned if you don't. ~ Eleanor Roosevelt

There are so many things we can do to build our confidence from avoiding behaviors that sabotage and the ways we're conditioned by society. What's more, there are things you can do to improve your self-confidence today. The reality is that the more self-confidence you have, the easier it is to do anything. Building your confidence is not a linear or a single-step process; it's an ongoing and ever-evolving one.

As we go through our days, we're constantly exposed to different emotions and experiences — some of which are positive, others negative — and all of these can impact your interactions with others. The more you build up your confidence, the more you'll be able to deal with the challenging situations that life brings.

One of the key challenges facing us as human beings is how to handle difficult situations in our lives without feeling like quitting or giving up. The truth is that most people don't like those "funny feelings" they get when they're heading towards something difficult!

What's the problem with feeling nervous?

If you're anxious about the possibility of failure, why even try in the first place? Believe it or not, there are plenty of successful people who have felt a similar level of nervousness and anxiety. Sometimes these feelings are strong enough to stop us from taking any action at all. It makes sense: if you really want to achieve something but you feel like giving up or failing, it's probably smarter to just stay in your comfort zone.

One way to get past the fear of failure is to take small steps and enjoy them. Focusing on smaller chunks of your day may seem low-risk, but it's a very powerful way of building confidence and inner strength. When you take those little steps, you'll find that it really takes less time than you think. And the more times you manage to do this, the more comfortable you'll become with taking action.

Our main challenge is that we're afraid of being wrong, and we don't know how to handle it in constructive ways to keep from making mistakes. Thinking we'll fail has a lot to do with teaching yourself to focus on all possibilities. There's no way of knowing the outcome of a decision until you make it. We always have options, and it's impossible to judge how things will work out in advance.

Relying incomplete ideas as a basis for thinking gives us an illusion of control, but it's not real. If you let go and look at things from another perspective, you'll find that your worries are baseless. The problem here is that our minds aren't making decisions; they're simply copying thoughts from society and other people. These are the things impacting your confidence, and you may not even know it.

How to combat fear of failure?

We've established that it's important to understand that you can't always predict the outcome of your decisions. In fact, it's impossible. The only way to get better at making decisions is to do it more often!

Another way to overcome this fear is to become more aware of what you're thinking. Having a reputation for having lots of knowledge can be helpful, but have you ever considered that your high expectations might be holding you back? No one can know everything in life! You may find yourself getting tied up in a lot of knots if you insist on knowing the perfect answers for every situation.

Stop judging yourself by what you "should" do. Perhaps you've even been told that you should study harder, earn more money, or look better. However, there's a great power in deciding for yourself how to live your life. If you let this drive your decisions, it's no wonder if you feel under pressure at times. Letting go of these rules may be an uncomfortable process, and it certainly won't be easy at first. When we learn about the ways we've been misled by society into believing certain things about ourselves, it can create anxiety and doubts about the choices we make and the paths to follow in life.

You'll see one of the foundations that leads to confidence is understanding how you've been influenced by society and can easily fall into believing the same things. The most important thing when it comes to our self-confidence is accepting who we are.

You can't change anything in your life that is not part of your self-concept. You can try to change a lot of things, but if they don't fit with who you are, they won't improve your confidence level! You need a good dose of self-belief, which will in turn help you become more confident as an individual.

<u>Stop being afraid of failure: it's inevitable to have our decisions go wrong.</u> We can't know exactly what will happen to us until we make our choices. You have to accept that sometimes you don't always make the right choices, and you can build your confidence by learning how to cope with failure. Failing at something doesn't mean you're a failure as a person. You'll find that throughout your life you'll go through a lot of mistakes and learn how to deal with them. So stop worrying about your mistakes! If you're able to learn from these experiences, then in time, most of them will turn into useful lessons for other things.

<u>Being honest with yourself is important</u>: Sometimes people are afraid of their own potential. They lie to themselves and think that they'll be happier if things stay the way they are. By

stopping yourself from reaching your potential, you're actually punishing yourself and reinforcing self-doubt. You're making excuses and creating lies in your mind, which will stop you from improving and moving forward in life!

If you're not honest about what you need to improve, you can't move forward. You'll build more effort into these negative forms of thinking, and it will be very difficult to break the cycle. So stop being so worried about who you are!

Nobody knows who you are better than you, and nobody can be as honest with you as yourself. That's why it's your responsibility to be careful about what thoughts come into your head. If you're not honest, it's easy to make mistakes and ponder scenarios in your mind that aren't true at all. In short, you can learn how to be a more confident person. Life is a rollercoaster of highs and lows, and there are certain things in life that people find difficult. "What if I fail?" is the question we all have at some point in our lives.

On the same note, we all feel uncertain about ourselves. These are temporary feelings of insecurity that you have to get over eventually. They'll pass if you keep your head on straight because it's only a matter of time until they disappear (so don't let them make you sad!).

Confidence is built from little steps moving forward each day. It comes from experience and knowledge, and it can be gotten by learning how to deal with situations better than others. This is something the world's greatest leaders learn how to do. To become more confident, you'll need to have faith in yourself and believe in your abilities. You'll need to constantly strive for growth and change, which will keep you from getting stuck in a rut and feeling like a failure.

Become a leader by learning how to build confidence: certain things are better than others, but it all depends on the situation you're in. There's no point thinking about what other people think of you, if they envy you or whatever it is they say behind your back.

Tap into the positive things in your life that really matter and stop focusing on the petty lies that other people try to convince you are true.

The truth is that it's not what others think of you that counts, it's what you think about yourself. Confidence comes with maturity, and maturity comes with time. If someone doesn't have a lot of confidence when they're young, it's probably because they haven't had enough experience to figure out who they want to be or how they want to act. Start by focusing on being confident in yourself right now at this very minute. You don't have to be perfect; you only have to do your best.

Don't compare yourself to others: We often see others who are more successful, attractive, or even wealthier than us. Does this make us want to emulate their lifestyle? Or does it make us want to be less successful, unattractive, or poorer? You might be thinking, "but if I were like them I could have ____" but if you compare yourself to others, you'll never feel better about yourself. Whenever you try and compare your life to other people's lives, you're missing out on the best parts of your life. Focus on how happy you are with yourself right now and how amazing your life is instead.

Don't criticize yourself: Don't get mad at yourself when you make a mistake, and don't even let anyone else talk bad about you. Remember that it's not your fault, but rather the fault of those who were rude and made you feel this way. I know it's hard to put yourself in the other person's shoes but try and understand what they were thinking without getting angry. All it will do is make them feel bad, which will just feed their negativity towards you.

Don't take criticism too seriously: One of the things that you might find yourself doing is letting other people's opinions bother you to the point where you feel self-conscious. This is a hard habit to break, and it's been known to happen to everyone at some point. But try and remember that not everyone shares your opinion about what's right or wrong, and with that in mind, try not to let their comments seriously affect your self-esteem too much.

You're probably aware of the fact that most people are insecure sometime in their lives. You might be wondering why, and you probably want to know how to get past it. There are so many things we take for granted in our lives, and some of us go through life feeling there's something missing.

Stop comparing yourself to others: The fact is we're all different, and there's no point in comparing yourself with someone else to find out what you're "lacking" in self-confidence. We're all different, and that's a good thing. There's no point in trying to be like anyone else because that's just going to hold you back from being who you truly are. You'll notice straight away when you start taking the right steps that your confidence will start to build up naturally over time. You'll also notice that other people become more accepting of you in front of others; this will get their attention, so they'll want to talk to you more.

Do what makes you happy and stop worrying about what other people think of your actions. If they're jealous of your success, then more power to them! If you want to improve your self-confidence, start by learning how to deal with yourself and the events in your life that might be making you feel down. You can't always change what other people say to you; sometimes they're just being rude! But you can change the way you react. Your personality is unique and special. Be proud of who you are, even if it isn't perfect yet.

Stop imposing your thoughts onto others: With today's exponential pace of social networking, we've basically started living in an era where we're always "on." It can be difficult to find time to just relax and not think about posting the next status update. And while your social media accounts are great channels of communication, it's important to remember that they aren't the only ones.

You should also try and stop imposing your thoughts onto other people as much as possible. Even if you're in a public setting, there's no need to always comment on what other people are doing or say. This will lead them feeling agitated and annoyed, so it's best just to keep quiet or ask a question instead of putting your two cents in when it isn't necessary.

Go outside and be with friends! We're all grown adults, but sometimes we forget that life is supposed to be fun! Life has a way of beating us down and making us feel bad about ourselves without really doing anything about it. It's important to remind yourself every once in a while you should enjoy yourself instead of spending so much time feeling sorry for yourself, thinking about what's happened in the past or worrying about what could happen in the future. When you're spending time with friends or even just by yourself, really focus on what's going on around you.

Listen to your intuition: Maybe you've heard it a million times, but I'm going to say it again – you're you and that's awesome!

Anyone who tries to make you feel less about yourself is just jealous, don't even take the time to think about them! We all have things in life that we'd like to improve. There are things other people have that we want for ourselves. But the truth is you can't focus on what's going wrong with your life or what's missing, as there are plenty of other things in your life that are already going well. You just have to realize that they are the good things and worth appreciating. To build self-confidence, you have to set goals for yourself, make the time to achieve them, and congratulate yourself when you get there. You might not be able to control what other people think of you, but you can take steps to become a more confident person and stop feeling so insecure about who you are.

Don't dwell on the past: There's a saying, "misery loves company," so if one person is feeling down it makes sense that others in their company feel down as well. The same thing works for happiness, so if someone is happy, others will be happy as well. Being surrounded by people you like and in a good mood can have a positive effect on you.

This kind of happiness tends to be contagious, so if you hang out with people who like to complain about things, it's hard not to feel down when they start bringing up the negative things affect their lives. It might sound strange, but when you spend time with someone who is complaining about something terrible going on in their life, it's easy to empathize. The next time you're feeling down, think of something you're happy about so that your mind will get stuck in a good place.

Stop thinking negative thoughts: The secret to becoming more confident is to stop thinking negative thoughts. You can't control what other people think or say about you, but you can control the way you think about yourself and react. If you start thinking negative thoughts, you'll feel like a failure in the eyes of others. You might think this is what other people are thinking about you, but it's not; it's something only you thinks about yourself. If someone criticizes your actions, don't pay attention to it. There's no point in getting upset; they're obviously just jealous of the good things that are going on in your life, trying to find ways to make their own lives seem better than yours.

Think positive: It's hard not to have thoughts about things that haven't necessarily gone as planned for us recently. The reality is that we all have both good and bad things that have happened to us and as difficult as it can be to just let those things go, it's the best thing for our mental health.

We always think about the worst thing that can happen – so let's think about the good things instead! If you're feeling down today, then think about what could make you feel better like a big slice of chocolate cake or even a nice bath! These people are petty if they are jealous of you because your life is going well. It's uncharacteristic of them to be happy for someone else when they aren't happy themselves. Their jealousy is just an expression of their inferiority complex.

Life can be difficult. You might feel down or maybe you've had some bad things happen to you. But remember that it's up to you how you handle these things. Make sure that these things don't affect your self-confidence. You're the only person who can take the necessary steps to become a more confident person and be who you really want to be.

You have that within you, but it's up to you if you're going to use it or not. Live for now!

Chapter 7:
Why do we Need Self-confidence to Succeed?

C onfidence is the key to success: if you don't believe in yourself, why should anyone else? The most successful people in the world never would have never reached that level of success without a strong sense of self-confidence. Think about it — do you really think that Gandhi or Leonardo da Vinci would have had any influence on history if they didn't believe in themselves? Probably not. Achievers are passionate about what they do, and they have a strong sense of purpose. They refuse to give up, even when it seems all is lost. They believe in their goals so much that failure is not an option.

However, the most successful people in the world were once just like you and me. They didn't always have a lot of confidence, yet they still succeeded! Thus, it's never too late to develop a sense of self-confidence and start believing in yourself.

Advantages of building self-confidence

In addition to the characteristics that accompany self-confidence, there are other reasons why self-confidence is important.

1. Self-confidence allows you to believe in yourself and your abilities despite any objections you may receive or ideas you may find "stupid": It's always easier to believe in yourself when

others want to discourage you. It's also easier when someone says something that offends or displeases you. But if you don't believe in yourself, how can you take those things personally? No matter what anyone else says, it doesn't change the fact that YOU have the ability to succeed and make your dreams come true.

2. Self-confidence allows you to look forward to the future rather than dwell on the past. Say you took a test in school and got a bad grade on your first try. You might think, "I'll never get a good grade in this subject," or "I'm not good enough for college." But if you believe in yourself, you can say things like, "Next time I'll study harder, so I get an A. Then I'll be able to go to college!" Dwelling on your past can prevent you from enjoying the present or planning for the future. In other words, don't let what happened yesterday control what happens tomorrow.

3. Self-confidence allows you to be happy: if you believe in yourself, you will be confident in your decisions. You know that where you are is the right place at this moment. And when you have self-confidence, you can enjoy whatever it is that makes life worth living.

How to build your sense of self-confidence

Now that we know why we need self-confidence and what advantages it gives us, let's try to figure out how we can develop a good sense of self-confidence. This might sound hard if you don't have self-confidence already, but just remember — it's never too late! These tips should help:

1. Develop a positive attitude: be genuine and be yourself. It's important to understand that the first impression you make when meeting someone is important. Even if you approach something positively, your initial impression can make all the difference. For example, if you walk into a store and say, "I don't like this store; it's boring." The person behind the counter might think you're being difficult or uncooperative and may get frustrated with you. By contrast, if you walk into the same store and say, "I love this store; I've been looking for a nice shirt for my dad for months!" Your attention will be drawn immediately to all the different products in that store — not just to those that are expensive or fancy.

2. Know what you want to achieve: you can't develop self-confidence until you know your goals. So, what are you trying to accomplish? What are your dreams and why are you going after them? Make a list of the things that matter most to you. Then ask yourself, "What do I want to be able to do in the future? What will provide me with my greatest sense of success?" If there is a specific goal you think is impossible, don't give up! Try to think outside the box and come up with new ways of reaching your goal. An example might be, "I want my little sister to be as happy as I am. But she can't be happy because

she's always in trouble. I'll have to find a way to get her out of trouble, and then somehow make her happier than I am."

3. Try something new: maybe you're not sure exactly what your goals are yet, but you're too afraid to try anything new. If this is the case, pick one small goal you are willing to try. Maybe it's riding a bike or making friends with the person at work who seems like he doesn't want to talk to anyone. Work on this goal over time until it becomes part of your daily routine. After this happens, think about taking on a new goal.

4. Believe in yourself: the most important thing you can do for yourself is to believe you can succeed even when things are tough. We all have bad days and bad times, but if we believe in ourselves, we'll always be able to get up and try again tomorrow. Try to remember the last time you were successful at something. If you're having a hard time, think of an experience where you felt like a winner. Remember how good it felt when it was all over? That's the way it will feel if you accomplish your goal. Just keep in touch with that feeling and use it to guide you.

5. Build your self-confidence: you can't expect to be confident without taking risks, especially when those risks mean failing in front of others. Take risky chances but build up self-confidence along the way by accomplishing small goals that feel uncomfortable or new. When you met your first friend, you felt embarrassed, but it made you feel so good that you wanted to

tell everyone about it. You developed self-confidence from that day on.

6. Trust yourself: if someone is doing something you don't agree with or don't think is the right thing to do, it's up to you whether or not to follow them. Remember how proud you felt when you followed your own goals and made all those new friends? Now remember how much fun you had when they did exactly what they wanted and weren't worried about what anyone thought of them? That's self-confidence, and sometimes following your heart means standing up for what's right even if no one else agrees.

A Positive Attitude is the Key to a Happier Life

These six tips are simple, but they are absolutely essential to get through challenging times. You can achieve anything you put your mind to; it's all in how well you approach things. Be positive and work hard — it'll pay off in the end!

Chapter 8:
Self-confidence tests

I t is not a secret that we all can feel low and want to improve our self-confidence. We might feel that we are not smart enough, successful enough or attractive enough. And this feeling of "lack" can be really hard to overcome even if we realize what is wrong (sometimes it's just problem in general). So, what can we do?

We all know how we can see "bad" with ourselves on the basis of various experiences and emotions. Of course, we can be really careful and considerate about every step in our lives, but still these feelings might exist. There are statements from other people, our own thoughts or maybe even situations that make us feel bad about ourselves. There is nothing wrong with these feelings; some are natural and useful to help us correct our bad habits. But what can we do if we have a lot of bad habits and feel bad about ourselves because of our inability to control our emotions?

More and more psychologists (for example, A. Ellis) consider that the easiest way to be happy is to build self-confidence and overcome personal issues. We might agree with this but still be unsure how it could help us. Let's look at an example: imagine that you are going out with your friends after being busy with important stuff. The weather is wonderful, and everyone seems to have enough energy to walk around the center of the city. But, suddenly, you realize that you don't feel good in the new dress you have just bought. You don't like it because of its color or style. It was too expensive, and you might feel guilty, but your friends seem to like it and ask for a photo.

So what do you do? Do you act as if everything is fine? Or do you want to be honest but still kind? Of course, the answer lies within you, but here is where self-confidence comes into play: it helps us make decisions that help other people feel better about themselves, too.

We can be honest in our feelings but still think about it more positively: "Maybe it's not that bad of a dress in general. It's just that I don't like the colour that much." This way we are able to escape all the bad things we might have thought about the dress and start thinking more positively about ourselves. This little change could make us feel good and even give some space for a new, more positive attitude.

There are many situations like this in our lives: if you see yourself as bad or flawed, try to reconsider your situation and thoughts. Maybe it's not you who is bad but the situation that needs some improvement. Eventually, this will help you feel good about yourself and build the self-confidence needed in other situations.

Some people say that they have low self-esteem because of their personality. They might find themselves too sensitive or become depressed over the tiniest events. But the reality is that we all are different and even if some features like sensitivity make us feel bad about ourselves, it doesn't mean that we shouldn't use this feature to make other people feel good about themselves.

Actually, if we feel bad about something, we can use it to our advantage in some situations. For example, I have a friend who has a lot of friends but can't stand it when someone stays with her for too long and asks for too much attention. But she has learned how to use this extreme sensitivity as an asset: she just stops talking to the person for a time or changes the subject to make the person feel better and motivated to do something else - without any negative emotions attached. Using such skills might seem difficult at first but with practice. you will be able to build your self-confidence further and further.

Some of us might have problems related to being too negative and it hard to believe this could be an asset. But imagine a situation where you are trying to encourage someone and suddenly realize that your own words are the right ones because they encourage you as well. So your words encourage other people, and since they feel better about themselves, they might try to achieve exactly what we need.

We can use our negativity: if we feel bad about ourselves, we can think about how bad other people feel or how bad the world actually is and start feeling more positively about our own situation. This will make us feel better about ourselves and will build self-confidence.

So, how can we fix bad habits? If you have such problems, try to understand why you don't want to change. Do you really want to change? The answer might be "no", but still it is important to think of the reasons. Once you have understood these reasons, try to think about how important they are for you and whether they could be useful in other situations. Of course, sometimes we really need to make some changes because we can't do anything else than this: maybe this is your case right now. But if your other options are more important, you can try to look for other solutions. If you are really stuck in a situation and you don't want to change anyway, the best thing to do is to work on your mindset and make yourself feel better about the situation.

We can try to change something in every aspect of our lives, even if it is only a habit, because our habits are the things we can do every day without thinking about them; and sometimes our habits are not good at all. So let's make better habits to finish all our problems, starting with the little ones.

Our small problems make us feel bad about ourselves and our situations, but later on these same situations might help us in other aspects of our lives. These kinds of situations are not as easy to understand as one big problem. Small problems can build self-confidence.

If we have too many problems, they make us feel bad and we can't think about any of them. But when we have only a few, they may seem easier to solve. At least, we can solve one of them. Since solving one problem will make us feel better, this will help us solve the next problem, or at least give us some more energy to continue further.

When we understand why we have a problem like this in the first place, it will be easier to solve it because we will have some understanding of our habits and therefore of our lives. We can only develop good habits if we understand them better; otherwise, they will stay with us and everything in our lives will remain the same.

Sometimes, when we set big problems for ourselves, we are able to solve only a part of them. But if other things happen at the same time or if other people have the same problems, then suddenly these big problems turn from blessings into disasters: they become useless and even harmful.

Chapter 9:
Positive Thinking and the Law of Attraction

I t's been said that we are what we think. If that's true, then why not think positively? That doesn't mean all bad thoughts need to be avoided. They can be used as a tool or lever when you want something bad enough to manifest it in reality. For example, you want to change your body. So in order to change it, you use negative thoughts or emotions like anger and frustration. It's not an easy task, because the brain is a powerful tool that helps us focus on the negative rather than the positive. However, if you take a lot of small steps towards feeling healthy, it will eventually get easier as you move forward.

If I think negatively about being overweight, I feel bad about myself, and my bad feelings start manifesting into reality. I eventually gain weight or stay overweight because I've been thinking negatively for so long. If I think negatively about myself, I'll never be happy. Once I start thinking positively, then everything will be great, and I'll be happy all the time.

This is a powerful thought that gets you to focus on something else and avoids acknowledging the problem or negative situation. While it sounds plausible, it is a lot of work to think positively! It takes effort to control your thoughts without feeling frustration over not being able to control things completely. You have an option to think differently.

Self-Confidence

If you are dealing with a fear of being overweight or not liking your body, you do have a choice. You can think about it and become frustrated. You can do what most people do and express rage, anger, or frustration because there is nothing to do about it but complain. The best way to avoid this from happening is to ignore the problem by thinking positively. It's just that simple. Don't focus on the negative and think about only about the positive instead.

Say the Law of Attraction is not working for you. It is not telling you to be positive, and we know that thinking positively is a way to make everything better and easier to handle, but it has a way of making things worse if you are not careful.

You need to find a balance between thinking about yourself realistically and positively at the same time. You need to accept that it will take some work to get good at, but it's doable with practice. You need to ignore negative thoughts like anger, frustration, or hopelessness as they will only make the situation worse regardless of how big or small they are. Instead of spending your time thinking bad things, why not think good things instead.

You can focus on negative things as a way to get rid of them or you can use them as a lever to manifest something better. It sounds like an excuse for someone who is overweight or doesn't like their body. It's not an excuse; it's a way of thinking you need to accept if you want to convince yourself that it's possible to change your body and be happy as a result. You have the ability to do this because you are the one who gives off life! As long as you have some form of positive energy flowing through you, you have enough power to make changes in your life. You are the one with the ability to create new ideas, even if they don't seem possible at first. You have enough power to come up with a million and one solutions as to how you wish your life would be.

Remember, this may not work for everyone or in every situation (challenges), but it's definitely worth trying if you're having a hard time dealing with your weight or body image in general. It's worth a shot because you will get better at it! As you go along and make new changes, so will your brain. You will eventually learn how to think about yourself differently and stay positive instead of feeling bad all of the time. It will get easier as time goes on and things happen. It may take some work to overcome your fears, but you will succeed as long as you keep trying.

Positive Thinking

First of all, think about these four things:

Believe in yourself

Trust in the law of attraction

Be kind to yourself

Don't compare yourself to others when it comes to body image or anything else for that matter

What's good for one person isn't good for everyone else so just be who you are and don't judge it either way. See things from a positive point of view. Keep these four things in mind and you'll be fine.

You are the one that's doing the attracting! It's up to you to make or break this law on thought. If you want it bad enough, you will find a way out of your problems; and if you don't, well, you will continue to have the same problems over and over. The bottom line is that as long as you remain positive about everything, nothing will stop you from reaching your goals. Not friends, family, yourself, or anyone else can tell you otherwise. It is all just a means to an end, the end being your happiness.

This law on thought works on the principle of attraction. It's like saying, "I'm positive; therefore I will succeed" or "I'm going to attract positive things into my life through my thoughts." You can attract dollars, or you can attract something that may seem worthless to some people but is priceless to you.

The keyword here is "attract". You have to believe that you will succeed in your endeavors before anything happens. The fact that you believe in yourself can only attract what you want toward you. The law of attraction is something that works for anyone who tries, and it helps us get what we want out of life. But the big question here is how do we know what we really need out of life?

You have a deeper understanding than most people think about what you really need or want in life. You already know if something will benefit you or not, so don't let anyone tell you otherwise unless it goes against your beliefs. You've just got to believe in yourself before anything else.

Think Positively

Now comes the most important part of this law on thought and that is to think positively. The fact that you believe in yourself is what is going to attract everything you need, so thinking positively can only help the process.

Thinking positively allows you to do more with your life by helping you reach your goals and dreams. – Demian Wells, self-help expert, motivational coach, and founder of Hot Singles Date Club

Think about every negative thing that has happened in your life up till now and try to come up with a solution to get over it. If you can do that, you are already on your way to making it happen. For example, if your ex-boyfriend cheated on you, think about the fact that you want to get over him; still thinking about him cheating will only stop the process. You have to think positive in order for it to work.

Think of what the future will bring and how happy you are going to be knowing that things have turned out well and that everything is going great for you. As long as that is what's going through your mind at any given moment then you should be good from there.

How to Make Your Own Happy Place

This is very important to get the law of attraction on your side. It's something you should work on daily, and if you do it right, you will start seeing results quite soon. What I mean by a happy place is your personal haven where nothing negative can bother you and where you are safe from all sorts of danger or negativity. While some people prefer calm mountains or beaches, others think of their favorite spot in the house and imagine it as their own happy place where they feel good about themselves.

To achieve your goal, relax your body and mind. To relax your mind, you can start thinking of a place where you feel great about yourself. Make sure there are no people around and that setting is unique for you. It can be any place, but it needs to feel good. Once you create your happy place, start imagining yourself in it. If the image is unclear or not very appealing, try to imagine it in more detail and eventually make it perfect. Try to immerse yourself into the scene for as long as possible, but try not to analyze it. Your happy place needs to be something you can do on a daily basis.

To relax your body, start running, dancing and you will suddenly become calm and relaxed. Laugh when you see something funny. Laugh at the funny things in life, but always do it with a positive attitude and never laugh at people for no reason. Smiling is a powerful tool for making friends, but if it's used inappropriately, then avoid smiling unless you want to look like an idiot. You need to treat this like anything else in your life to keep yourself motivated.

Positive thoughts will attract positive things into your life. – Demian Wells

Start thinking positively and you will start to feel better about yourself sooner than you imagine, but it's not that simple. It won't happen overnight so be patient and realize that the process is worth the rewards that come at the end. This is how things work so make sure you are ready for any challenge or obstacle that comes your way on the road to getting healthy and happy.

Focus on Your Needs

To change something, you need to first focus on what you want and then think about what needs to be changed. You have a choice on where the focus of your attention should stay with regards to your goals. It's up to you whether it is your body or some other aspect of life that is troubling you. If you want to lose weight, then think about what you need to do to reach your goal. If you want more money, think about what needs to be changed – like your career or location. If your health is affected by something serious, focus on it and try to make the necessary changes for it not to happen again. It's a process that works because you must learn how to focus on yourself and see what will benefit you the most in the long run. This is a great law that helps us think positively about whatever we want, but there are things that we shouldn't ignore either.

It's important to involve other people if you want things to work. Take your family for example. If your family is not supportive of the way you are living, you will have a hard time getting what you want because they will push against you and tell you why what you want is impossible or laughable. This makes it hard to achieve success, but it doesn't mean that it's impossible. There are different ways of looking at situations so don't let anyone tell you otherwise when bringing up bad ideas or comments about what's going on in your life. This law on thought works for any situation and this is why it's important to know when to accept help. There's a difference between something that can be done on your own and something that is too big of a challenge to accomplish alone. This applies to anything from losing weight, getting a promotion at work, or even getting out of debt. You may have the power but if you don't know how, you'll have no idea where to start. Let someone help so the change can go more smoothly.

That's how things work in life and things are not always as they appear. Focus on the small things that make a big difference. Know when to accept help and when not to let other people tell you what to do or think. Make sure you are following your dreams and not anyone else's. They don't live the same life as you so they can't possibly judge what's best for you. If you want something done right, then do it yourself! If not, find someone who's willing to help because it might be impossible for things to get better.

Power of Thought

You think on a daily basis so how do we think about what we want in life? The only way we know how to think is by using our five senses - sight, hearing, smell, taste, and touch. We live in a world with many smells, sights and sounds that we don't even realize at times, but it is different with thoughts. Thoughts are a form of power. We think all the time about many different things, and this is how we focus our attention on what we want. It's how we can get things done in our lives and that's why it's important to train your mind the right way. about whatever you want in life. Begin by training your mind each day to think positively so you can reach your goals easier. Start thinking positively so you become a good role model for other people.

You want to change things so make sure you do it in the right way and lose weight the healthy way.

Remind yourself on a daily basis of what you want or need to get things working for you. You don't have to believe in something all of the time because this is not magic. But it's a great way to gain mind control because it can keep your mind focused on the task at hand like losing weight or ending bad habits. It is important to stay focused, but it's not something that you can always do. Sometimes a distraction comes up and you need to let go of your focus on what you want because if you don't, then it will be difficult for things to get better.

You're trying to concentrate, and it seems like nothing is working out, so you give up. It helps if you have a plan in place so when the time come, it's something that looks easy and works at the same time. We can make it happen if we want, so focus on what you want and try to ignore any distractions that come your way.

Focus on yourself and be as happy as you can because life is only as good as you make it. If you are happy, there is no reason for anything to go wrong. You have a choice to make in order for things to get better. If this means letting go of something to achieve other goals, that needs to happen so everything will continue moving forward and you will stay on top of things.

The law on thought works for any situation. It doesn't matter how bad things get because things never stay the same forever, but there are times when we need to let go of something and focus on what we want. You should be thankful if you need to let go of something bad to get over it.

The Focus Should be on Happiness

Your mind has the ability to focus at any given moment. If you're trying to complete a project, your mind will focus on it, and you won't think about anything else until it's done. This is a good thing because it helps us get the job done but sometimes, we need to focus on something completely different for things to start looking up. It can be something that makes us think about the way we live and wonder what we're supposed to be doing with our lives. The only way to do this is if we have something else that requires our attention. It's very important because if you're not happy, there's no reason for you to want to do anything else. You need to focus on what you want and make sure you're ready for anything that comes your way.

We need to work on a positive outlook towards our lives to make it better. To start off, you can change your thoughts at any given moment so things will begin to look up for you and go the right way as they are supposed to. This is more than just focusing on what you want because it also means thinking about how happy you should be in life. If you must focus on the serious thing in your life, make sure that you do it in the right way, so it won't bring you down.

This means choosing what makes you happy and sticking with it because if not, his can lead to depression and sadness which are not the best things in life. If we're not happy, then there is no point of doing anything else. This can make it hard for us to get out of bed each morning. When we get out of bed in the morning, then everything becomes possible so we don't let anything stop us. Life is a beautiful thing and if you want to experience it to the fullest, follow some of these laws on thought because they are very important for anyone who wants to keep moving forward. If you don't focus on what you want and what makes you happy, then life will pass you by and there will be so much that you'll miss. You need to take a break from focusing so much on the serious things in life because it's important to make a change when we need to. It doesn't matter how hard something is going to be because we can always get it done if we try harder. When a distraction happens, you need do something different. It might mean you need to let go of something or you have to focus on something important to make things better for everyone. It helps us get through our lives easier when we have a clear head and can think about what we want. If we're happy with our lives, there is no reason why we shouldn't be able to accomplish anything. This includes making more money, getting a promotion at work, or losing weight for example. It's important to put your focus on the right things in life because it will help you think of what you need to be doing to experience something better.

Chapter 10:
How to Use Visualization to Create the Life of Your Dreams

V isualization is a simple technique to create the life of your dreams regardless of who you are or where you live. It works 100% of the time, every single time! It is a method that anyone can use to improve their life in any way they desire, and it only requires the power of your own mind. By using this method properly, it will bring about changes in your life that may even startle you. You will begin to attract whatever you want quite easily with little or no effort at all. You can do this from anywhere in the world, and you do not need anyone's permission.

What is Visualization?

Simply put, visualization is a technique where you close your eyes and create a very clear image in your mind of what you want to have happen in your life. It can be anything at all like finding a new car or winning ten million dollars. It can be as simple as getting a better job and having a nice house to live in. You just imagine having what gives you the most pleasure. The most important thing is that you think about it and really believe in what it will be like. You will find that you will come very close to real life soon after the process of visualization begins.

The Power of Visualization

What most people do not realize is that visualization can create any result you desire, whether or not the results are what you had imagined. This may sound a bit unbelievable at first, but I have proven over and over through the use of this technique that it is true in every single case. It is necessary to explain in a bit more detail. You are not limited to the things you see in your day-to-day world. You can imagine things that may seem impossible to the average person. When you start using visualization, you will begin to see your mind at work every day, and it will amaze you at what it is capable of doing.

The Power of Your Subconscious Mind

When you use visualization techniques on a regular basis, your subconscious mind will begin working directly for you instead of against you as it does in most people. It will take the desires you hold and use them to serve your best interests. Your subconscious mind is always listening to all the thoughts you have while you are awake and asleep. It can only pick up on thoughts you want it to pick up on, and it will go out of its way to do so. You may not get anywhere near what you want in life, but by improving your visualization skills with this method, the results will become much more obvious over time.

How to Use Visualization to Create the Life of Your Dreams

Over time, visualization can become an integral part of your life. When you have a problem, you can close your eyes and see the way to solve it right in front of you. When you want to learn something new, it is easy to see it in your mind as if you were actually there. When a person feels restricted or limited by circumstances, they need only think about seeing a change in their life and the problem will be gone. You do not have to dream up situations that are completely impossible; simply think about what is possible and then make it happen.

I have found that people who do not use visualization on a regular basis tend to get frustrated at times with their situation or lack of results in life. They think there is something wrong with them or their methods, as though they are doing the wrong thing. They use the excuse, "I am just not trying hard enough" or "I thought that I was supposed to get that, and I still don't have it." This goes to show where people's mindsets have gotten them. People do not take action because they do not want to waste their time. The most important thing is learning how to visualize and then take action.

An Example of Using Visualization to Create the Life of Your Dreams (Law of Attraction)

You may be interested in buying a car and you drive by a dealership. You see it, it looks nice, and you walk inside. When you walk in the door, you are immediately attracted to the vehicles for sale. There is one in particular that attracts your attention more than the others on the lot. You find yourself standing there looking at this vehicle with total conviction that it is yours right now no matter what happens next. You are standing there enjoying the fantasy, and suddenly this vehicle in your mind becomes yours - and you walk out with it.

That scenario is a perfect example of what you can do in life with visualization, but it can get even better. Imagine that you have followed the above steps, but instead of walking out of the dealership with the vehicle, the one you really wanted all along was not for sale. You immediately go back to the dealership and stroll inside, thinking to yourself this time, "I am going to find out why I was not able to get this car earlier." You walk in, look at the vehicles, and once again they draw your attention to one particular model. You are standing there looking at one like it is going to jump up and run you over in a second, but you just know that this time it will work out. You can do this with any kind of situation and with any type of vehicle.

You could be standing in line at the cash register about to leave the store, and a model you have been thinking about buying all day appears on the TV screen behind the employee ringing you out. You walk straight back into that store, buy that item, and walk out feeling great about yourself.

You can even go back to that car dealership and get the car you "wished for". All of this may sound like a dream, but it is not. It is reality. You can do all these things and more with visualization, but I have to warn you that before doing this, go over your technique in detail with someone who knows what they are doing so you will not make a mistake in your efforts. Have fun and begin to prove to yourself that visualization really works for everyone no matter what the situation.

Visualization and the Power of Your Mind

The power of your mind is what makes you successful, rich, and happy. Your mind can make your life miserable if it goes in the wrong direction - so it is very important to keep it on course. You need to learn how to visualize for this to happen. What I want you to see from all of this is that visualizing helps you build wealth right now and in the future because it can increase your chances of winning as well as predicting the outcome of other people's chances. Visualizing can help you win at anything in life.

Now I am going to give you some examples of what I am talking about. One thing that many people do either consciously or subconsciously is they always try to win, even when they do not know exactly why. If you are playing the lottery, odds are that someone out there is already planning to win the entire jackpot. You may know this and also know it does not matter - so why not join them. The same goes for any other game you can think of playing where the outcome is uncertain. More than likely it will be good if it is played with the right attitude and technique.

What happens with many people is that they set the goal too high and expect it to happen in a short period of time. In this case, they feel discouraged and give up because it does not happen as expected. With visualization, you pick the amount of wealth you want to have at any point in your future life and then visualize getting there. This will encourage you to go after it and accomplish what was planned many months or years ago.

Develop a positive mindset

Feeling good about yourself brings the results you want. This can be done by exercising, eating healthy and even thinking good thoughts so you feel better about yourself. When you feel good about yourself, it makes it easier to attract health and wealth into your life.

Be ready for success even when you think things are going wrong. For example, if you have a plan to develop a business after graduation and your family does not believe in it, stay firm in your decision and know that the moment will come when they will assist. Be sure to stay positive and expect the best.

Visualize all your goals, and you may be surprised at the results. It is not possible to list all of the uses visualization can have in your life since everyone has different intentions and goals. I hope you were able to learn a lot from this chapter, especially about the power of visualization and how it can bring success right now regardless of who you are or what you do.

It may take some time to become a great visualizer, but anyone can do it with practice. I will now leave you to move on with your life and begin to use visualizing techniques in everything you do. Remember that this is a very powerful skill, so learn it and keep it for the rest of your life.

Chapter 11:
Positive Affirmations and Thoughts to Recover from Bad situations in Life

T his chapter is to help you recover from bad situations. The effects of these bad situations are complicated, and some people can't seem to get out of the hole they have dug for themselves. But don't worry, this is not going to be a challenge or something that's hard, because I'm here with you. I will help you avoid the pitfalls that can cause negative thoughts in your life and take you on the positive path.

First, let me talk about the effects of negative, painful thoughts on our bodies and emotions. Science has proven that most of our emotions are triggered by the brain. When unpleasant things happen, we immediately start experiencing feelings and problems. We also have our own beliefs about situations and those feelings are in our minds as well as in our bodies with a certain intensity. The more intense these feelings, the more pain we feel in a certain part of our body (for example, the stomach or chest). This pain is usually caused by disturbing messages coming from our brains. This can be a disastrous combination of negative thoughts and feelings, which results in self-doubt, uncertainty, fear, and anxiety.

So how do we deal with these unpleasant situations? How can we stop our bodies from reacting to negative thoughts and feelings? Well, we can start by changing the way we speak about ourselves in our minds. As said before, most of our disturbing emotions are caused by certain thoughts about the things that happen to us. For example, when we feel as if someone doesn't like us or is jealous, an image / thought comes to mind telling you this is so, and then you go into panic mode because you are feeling insecure. This is what creates the feeling of pain in the body. But you're also telling yourself that this is bad, but you should not feel this way (insecurity, jealousy, anger), which may seem like a contradiction.

Every thought has a vibration or energy, and it comes from the subconscious into the conscious mind. Because it's energy, it can't be wrong; it's just a different vibration. It consists of the thoughts about what we don't want to happen instead of what we do want to happen. So, if you start to think positive affirmations or positive thoughts about yourself when this bad feeling came up, you will change how you feel and therefore change the energy coming toward your brain.

This will make your brain start to believe and actually see a different or new picture / reality than what was there before. As you start to speak positive and happy thoughts, instead of negative thoughts about yourself, this will make your heart pump more warm blood into your body, making it feel better than ever.

Our brains are connected with our nervous system which is connected with all our other organs in the body. The brain changes the way we feel at the base level so we have to care for it. How? We can change the thoughts and feelings in our minds, so we don't get stuck in the negative vibrations. They can be changed into positive energy. You can do this by reading affirmations and positive thoughts about yourself and by practicing mindfulness. The first entails merely learning how to read them, while the second involves actively practicing their use.

You should start by reading affirmations. You may also try practicing mindfulness. You can do this by following these simple steps: sit down somewhere quiet. Close your eyes and put your hands on your lap, palms up. Now try to feel your body sitting on your chair or the floor you are sitting or lying on. Feel the temperature around you and think of this as a healing process for yourself. Start breathing deeper and slower than before, inhaling through your nose, and exhaling through your mouth. Feel each breath go in and out of your body as it happens. Watch your hands on your lap, try to feel each finger individually, including the thumb. Notice your body and think of it as a healthy whole – not just one part. Begin to follow your thoughts. You may start noticing your breathing echoing through you like a drumbeat.

Another technique is to write down what you think will be the outcome of a bad situation (it could be even an exercise). Positive affirmations are great for this because they allow you to speak positive things without having to worry about how other people perceive them. Here are some examples:

"I am confident in my looks."

"I am capable of doing what I want to do."

"I am secure with all the success I have."

"I am happy because I know that everything will be alright. All my doubts and fears are illusionary."

You can also write down negative situations and negative affirmations about them. Then rewrite them into positive ones. This should make your subconscious mind accept the new versions as true and therefore bring them to pass. You can also do this with people you don't even know who are important in your life. If you're struggling with something in that a friend or colleague is going through, it may be helpful to write down the negative thoughts / thoughts your friend has. Then rewrite those negative things into positive ones. This should make your subconscious mind accept the new versions as true and therefore pass them on.

By doing this, you will begin to experience improved energy and higher levels of health. Your body and mind will begin to work in a balanced way. You will feel more centered and find it easier to adapt to various circumstances. You will be more creative as well as speak your mind more openly without fear of being judged.

Come back to this page and read it again when you have time until you can recite it by heart. This new way of thinking should be applied to your whole life. You will start approaching everything differently, even when you are not thinking about it. It affects every aspect of your life. You will find yourself much more optimistic and happier than before. I personally recommend you keep the new approach of thinking about yourself as positive and realistic in your mind, even when certain negative situations come up. It is important to practice this in front of a mirror every now and then to really sink it in.

This will help you be more aware of your thoughts, which is crucial for thought manipulation. You can also experiment with making affirmations for the things that happen to you while having general "negative" thoughts (or vice versa). This helps you to be aware and control your thoughts. You can practice all the time no matter how good or bad the situation is. It should be a continuous work in progress. When you reach the point where the method becomes second nature, your whole life will start changing for the better! You will lead a more satisfying and rewarding life than ever before. You may even discover new talents and abilities previously hidden inside of you. Whatever it may be, at this point it is very important for you to take action now! Don't get stuck in analysis paralysis...just go ahead and do something!

Chapter 12:
Living in the Present Moment

S elf-confidence is a foundation for living in the present moment. If you are self-confident, you are capable of being fully alive. The average person lives only about 40% of his or her life in the present moment. Most people are mesmerized by their past and worry so much about their future that they miss what is happening now and experience it as an infinite time limit.

Living in the present means freedom from your past and fear of your future; it means overcoming grief, guilt, regret, shame, resentment, anger, sadness, and all other forms of suffering that exist solely in your thoughts.

For the most part, you live in ignorance of suffering that grows from moment to moment. You suffer from sadness about your past and anxiety about your future. You are worried about what has happened and whether it will happen again. Your mind is filled with regret, shame, and guilt. These thoughts make up all the suffering in your life. All that is left are fears of forgetting something, fear of not remembering some event or fear of missing out on something in the future.

Each time this happens, you lose partial control over your thoughts and feelings. You are no longer fully alive. You are caught in the past or the future, and you have a limited connection to what is happening NOW in your life.

When you accept the present moment for what it is, you gain control over your thoughts and feelings. You begin living fully in each moment because you know that there is nothing to worry about tomorrow. You live fully today because you know that there is nothing to feel guilty about yesterday. You are free of regret, sadness, anger, and fear as they only exist in your imagination and not reality. You are free of anxiety for when something good or bad is going to happen. Only your imagination creates these thoughts, and you can let go of them.

Instead of reacting to your thoughts, feelings, and emotions, you can respond nonreactively to how things have turned out. You live fully in the present moment because you are no longer caught up in intense emotion that can only be released by changing what you are doing or thinking. By not focusing on the past or the future, you take actions that produce a result right NOW. This produces an immediate change in your state of mind.

In short, you can create happiness by responding to your thoughts, feelings, and emotions. Your past and future manufacture these harmful thoughts, compelling you to constantly struggle with them. You are not responsible for them, however, no matter how much you want them to be.

You may have many thoughts about the past and future, but they are not real. The present moment is when real things happen in your life. Now is when you are fully alive because you know there is nothing to suffer from in the past or nothing to anticipate for the future. You are living in the moment and making your life happen.

You can be fully alive even when you are alone because it is an internal state that depends upon how much you accept the present moment. As long as you accept it, there is nothing to fear for there is always something to do about. In the present moment, you can make a decision to get up from where you and move to another location. You gain control over yourself and your environment when you live in the present because your mind and body become one unified force that predominately operates in the NOW. You become the author of your life experience instead of living in reaction to your past mistakes and fears of the future.

Self-confidence is essential to living in the present moment. You can be self-confident because your thoughts are in control and not reacting to other people's demands. Instead of being sad because something has happened, you get up, let go and move on to something else that needs changing. You would have continued to feel bad about it; but this is not true if you accept what has happened and move on.

As said, your past and future are in your imagination, not in reality. They are not true, but when you believe in them, they become real, and you can become caught up in them. You cannot change the past because it has happened; it has been recorded and happened whether you wanted it to or not. If you had done something wrong or something good, the experience is a part of your life story. Feelings about how it happened will be added to your story over time. The only way to change a bad experience into a good experience is by changing what is going on NOW. You can only change what you are doing and thinking in the present moment. Reactions to the past and future can be a cloud of negativity that can distract your attention.

Those who cannot let go of their past or future find themselves guilty for the negative experiences that have happened to them. This is another cloud of negativity created by how they react to the past or future. They suffer from guilt over what happened, not because it was real, but simply because they wanted it to be real. If they had done something different, things would have turned out different.

When you react to your past or future thoughts, feelings, and emotions, you are adding another layer of chaos to your experience because the real problem is not what happened – only what you are doing and thinking about it. The real problem is always too much fear, too much anger or too much sadness that had caused you to react in the first place. These clouds of negativity can be diminishing as you become more self-confident and self-reliant.

This requires accepting, living in the present moment, and letting go. When nothing bad happens, there are no negative experiences that need to be released. It is important to remember that if nothing happens, it is because you have chosen not to change anything and not because you have accepted what happens in the moment.

You can be fearless when you are self-confident and do not react to the past or future. If someone has hurt your feelings, you can accept that they may never apologized. You may never find out why they behaved in a way that was harmful to your feelings or why they didn't care about how their behavior affected your life in a negative way. They may never tell you or anyone else why they did what they did.

This does not mean that you cannot be happy. It just means that you have the freedom to make your own happiness, and you can begin to make it now. When you are self-reliant and self-confident, you will never react to the past or future because there is no fear of what has happened or no hope for a different future event. You are living in the present moment where life is taking place right now. You are free to be happy every moment that you choose to think positive thoughts.

Being self-confident and living in the present are powerful ways to deal with past and future events. Once you learn how to stop reacting to negative past or future experiences, you will notice that your life is filled with wonderful experiences, more happiness than negativity. You will find that you are living in the present moment, and you will be even more fulfilled than you ever thought possible.

You may wonder how you can learn to live in the present and let go of the past. This is an area where self-hypnosis can help. Have a session with a professional hypnotherapist who will guide you into self-hypnosis and allow your subconscious to become receptive to new ways of thinking about past and future issues. Reconnecting with your inner confidence can take time. However, you are worth the effort.

If you find yourself struggling with self-confidence, ask yourself what's missing in your life? Are you missing loving relationships? Do you lack the right job or career opportunity? If so, what can you do to fill these needs in your life and start building a foundation for future success? The answers may be simple and easy to achieve if you know how to use self-hypnosis for personal empowerment.

Chapter 14:
Setbacks and Risks

T he more you practice self-confidence, the better you will become at overcoming obstacles. If you feel like your self-confidence has decreased in the past few days, then take the needed steps to get it back. In order to get back on track, you can do things that help boost confidence such as changing your routine or ritual for a while, challenging yourself by trying something new, and setting achievable goals and making small victories happen through taking action—such as cooking an easy meal or saying hello to a stranger once a day—to build momentum. As you build your self-confidence, the more you will want to act on your impulses. The more you act, the more you will feel like yourself. The more you feel like yourself, the stronger your self-confidence will become.

Letting go of Perfection

Another key to building self-confidence is to be less demanding of yourself. Let go of striving for perfection. When we are perfectionists, we set the bar very high for ourselves, which often leads us to feel like we are always falling short. This can lead to disappointment and a lowered sense of well-being. If you are a perfectionist, simply asking yourself if this specific really matters so much can be an effective way to gain some objectivity and perspective on your situation.

Self-confidence is also about being more accepting of yourself. Often we can have serious self-esteem issues because we are very focused on how something could have been done better or by someone else in comparison to ourselves, rather than taking responsibility for the situation. If you are feeling low in self-confidence, instead of berating yourself for any mistakes, accept them instead of obsessing about them.

Often self-confidence issues can be caused by our beliefs about ourselves. We tend to think that individuals who look a certain way or have certain skills must also have superior qualities and abilities than those without these things. For example, because someone is tall and good looking, you think they must also be intelligent and have great interpersonal skills. Yet this is often not the case. In fact, many individuals who are considered attractive are actually very insecure themselves because they have been socialized to believe that these traits will lead to happiness and success. Then it doesn't always work out!

So if you base your self-confidence on outward appearance, you may feel insecure about the shortcomings in other areas of your life. The best way to dispel these beliefs is to practice gratitude for your own unique attributes, no matter how insignificant they might seem to others.

Understanding Your Perceptions

The most important factor behind a lack of self-confidence is our self-perception. Although on the surface it may seem that our perceptions are about something we know, in fact they are often based on misinterpretations. This happens all the time. For example, if you got a grade you were not happy with, you may have interpreted this as meaning you are bad at school and therefore bad at life. Yet this is simply not reality. It's easy to fall into this type of thinking pattern because our critical parent voice sounds just like an objective truth telling us what is really going on, when in fact it's just our own voice amplified and distorted via an overactive imagination or cognitive distortion. In order to be true to ourselves, we must have full awareness of our perceptions.

Sadly, many people do not understand this very basic concept because they have been taught that their parents or other authority figures (social media) have the answers; and if they don't, it's their fault for being clueless, misguided or even stupid. Many people have actually created their own limiting beliefs based on erroneous information from others without realizing it. The truth is nobody knows for sure what the world should look like or how we should act in it. We are each responsible for our own lives and understanding these concepts is imperative to living a fulfilling life filled with self-confidence.

When we understand the basics of our perceptions, we are able to make changes in the way we react in certain situations. We can also learn that blaming others for our own feelings is a waste of time and energy. It's not what happened to us in the past that causes us to feel a certain way today—though it may have at one point—it's how we perceive what happened and how it makes us feel now.

Self-confidence is basically about feeling comfortable with yourself in your current place and situation in life, regardless of circumstances. It is about acceptance instead of judgement based on your interpretation of self-worth. Even when we do feel judged, we can choose to use our minds to accept and respect those opinions without feeling bad because we know there is fundamentally no right or wrong way to be.

Improving Self-Confidence

There are many components to self-confidence: self-esteem, identity, personality, and attitude. These components are developed in different ways and at different times in life. Some people have to spend a lot of time getting these things just right, while others seem to have just figured out how they want themselves to be. Either way, we all can benefit from some self-improvement. Here are some tips:

1.) Practice Gratitude

Gratitude is the most powerful tool you have for improving your self-esteem and your self-confidence in general. The more grateful you are for what you have, the more self-confident you will feel. Think about it: the more grateful you are that someone saved your life, the more confident you will feel about saving someone else's life in the future . If we practice gratitude every day, we begin to see our lives as having infinite worth and possibilities no matter how bad a situation may seem at first glance.

2. Develop the habit of fully expressing yourself at least once a day, whether it is to a person or in a letter or note. The more comfortable you are with expressing your true self, the more confident you will be. The way you communicate with other people creates your first impression. You don't have to let others say or do anything that triggers negative emotions, but they are most likely occurring in the background when we get triggered. To bypass this trigger, write down your feelings and thoughts as soon as they occur so you can process them faster and gain control over your emotions rather than letting them control you.

3. Practice being present in the moment and engaged with what you are doing instead of worrying about the past or hoping for future successes.

4. Practice being sure of yourself by not accepting other's judgements and opinions of you. Know that others may think differently, but these opinions have nothing to do with you as a person and are not an accurate reflection of who you are. Feel good knowing that if you did make a mistake or mess up, it wasn't because something is wrong with you. People can accept

people for who they are, but we cannot force others to accept us for who we were.

5. Practice being spontaneous and doing things your way instead of going by the rules in a prescribed manner. If you are stuck in "If I do this, then it will look this way" thinking, ask yourself what would happen if you did something different. The more confident and secure you feel, the more spontaneous and interesting your life will become.

6. Practice expressing your gratitude to others daily.

7. Take notes on things you are grateful for and write them down.

8. Ask yourself if you are saying yes to opportunities, or if you are constantly saying no out of fear of doing well, being the center of attention or looking foolish?

9. Practice focusing on what is happening right now, not worrying about the future or taking things so seriously that they affect your ability to focus on the task at hand. If something is bothering you about a situation in the present, take a step back and assess it from a distance instead of allowing things to make you anxious or stressed out.

10. Spend some time on your own.

11. Spoil yourself and do something nice for yourself, because you deserve it.

12. Be sure to carve out personal time each week in which you can do something for yourself, to feel more positive about being single and having time to pursue your interests.

13. Take care of your body by eating well, exercising regularly, resting, and getting good quality sleep at night.

14. Fill up your life with activities you enjoy so you won't be sitting around dwelling on the fact that you're single when you could be doing something productive or fulfilling that would benefit your mind and spirit instead.

Conclusion

The most important takeaway from this book that we should all be striving for self-confidence. That doesn't mean you have to be perfect or view yourself as infallible, but you do need to act like a person who has achieved great things. Live your life with conviction and show people around you that you are somebody who deserves respect and admiration. Self-confidence is not an easy skill to master, but it will serve you well in every aspect of your life.

Self-confidence is one of the most difficult skills for anyone to master in life, but it's also very important if we want ourselves and our work taken seriously by others. Being self-confident means that you know you're a good person and can make major contributions to society. It means that others will see you as someone who knows what he or she is doing in life and has the potential to excel at it.

It's important for everyone to have self-confidence because we all need money (or at least we want it), friends (we want them), jobs (we need them), etc. If we don't feel like we're contributing to society and having a positive influence on the world, we may begin to question ourselves and our decisions. Then we go nowhere. Always look at yourself as a person who is making an impact. You won't be afraid of making mistakes because you know that others will have your back.

Look at the big picture and try not to focus on what you're doing wrong. When you do this, you will stop second guessing yourself in every little thing that happens in your life. If something isn't going well for you, look at it like an opportunity for growth rather than something that needs to be fixed right now.

That doesn't mean you've failed in any way. It just means that what's happening right now is a learning experience. Try not to let your emotions get the better of you in times like these because they can be deceiving and manipulative. They will try to tell you that something isn't going right because it never does, but self-confidence will stop us from thinking like this. So now you know how to get it!

CPSIA information can be obtained
at www.ICGtesting.com
Printed in the USA
BVHW092219300421
606210BV00004B/828

9 781914 527012